SPEAK

SPEAK WELL ENGLISH

AN GUIDE FOR ALIENS TO
SUCCESSFUL INTERCOURSE IN
THE CORRECTLY ENGLISH MODE

TOMAS SANTOS

Edited by T. A. CUTLER
Foreword by TONY HAWKS

Michael O'Mara Humour

First published in Great Britain in 2004 by
Michael O'Mara Books Limited
9 Lion Yard, Tremadoc Road
London SW4 7NQ

A CIP catalogue record for this book is available
from the British Library

ISBN 1-84317-088-4

1 3 5 7 9 10 8 6 4 2

Designed and typeset by Martin Bristow

Printed and bound in England by
Cox & Wyman Ltd, Reading, Berks

Uncover Tomas Santos bit more in his internest site:
www.tomassantos.com

I should like much devoted this book my mother and to my home land that I lived when I was infantile. It was the ground of milk and syrup. I darling it.

TOMAS SANTOS

About the author

Tomas Santos decided long ago to exchange the balmy climate of his homeland for the wet and wind of the British Isles, but it is only recently that circumstances have allowed him to settle in England. He has made his home in Hove, a popular seaside resort much favoured by retired gentlefolk, where he is a student at one of the town's language colleges.

Tomas Santos was motivated to write *Speak Well English*, he says, by a desire to improve on the 'incomprehending' [*sic*] phrasebooks currently in the shops. He has never written a book before and neither is his English especially good. Nonetheless he has worked doggedly on the project undaunted by his status as a complete beginner.

Tomas Santos enjoys an unusually wide variety of hobbies, including swimming, flying, and music. His band, Wind, String & Faggots, plays a lively role in the cultural life of his home town.

About the editor

After a number of false starts as a teacher, set designer, double-bass player, portrait painter, theatre usher, cartoonist, toyshop manager, printer, broadcaster, typographer, lyricist, wine waiter, film editor, puppet maker, media trainer, publications manager, speechwriter, magician, City analyst, magazine editor, TV executive, communications consultant, and sometime ghost writer for Cardinal Hume, T. A. Cutler left the rat race to spend more time with his slippers.

He describes the experience of editing *Speak Well English* as 'special', but the task has exacted a punitive toll on his morale and he is now on beta blockers 24/365.

T. A. Cutler lives near a windmill on the South Coast, where he has written the seminal *Tackling Self-Hatred: Anger Management for Hostile Depressives*, and is currently working on a memoir, provisionally entitled, *My Life of Sex and Violence*. He eats a diet rich in fibre and has one foot bigger than the other.

Contents

Foreword
by **Tony Hawks**

I first became aware of the existence of Tomas Santos when I received a letter from him which was waiting for me at the stage door at the Liverpool Everyman just before the final performance of the tour of my show *One Hit Wonderland*. As I relaxed in my dressing room, prior to my performance, this neatly addressed letter lay before me for some time before I opened it. One never knows what to expect from this kind of mail. Experience has shown that the content tends to range from fawning flattery to outrageous insults. Somehow I had the feeling that this letter was going to break new ground. Perhaps the clue lay in the way that the letter had been addressed:

Tony Hawks
In care: Everyman Theatre

I opened the envelope and reached inside, growing ever more inquisitive as to its contents. I was soon intrigued:
'Yesterday I came in my best trousers in the Corn Exchange, Brighton, to view yours show "One Hip Wonderland". I accompanied with my landlord duaghter and she insisted such that I must stop it to always exploring Wagner's "Ring" that I

must made more the relaxings shows. So I had done it with her!'

I was fascinated. The author of the letter didn't seem to have the fullest grasp of his chosen language of communication. He continued:

'Yours presentation was laughable.'

Yes, well I hoped I thought I knew what he meant. Then came an offer:

'Tony, you are the very musician that you can "titillate the ivory". Also you can strump the guitar. So I shall proposition you: I had assembled the music band in Brighton that we visit in the hospitals to ameliorate and to entertained the patient. Ours group is called Wind, String & Faggots. We have it the bags-pipe, drums (on the string), strumpets, hurdy-gurdy and some sackbuts. We require a president! Will you accept it the offer to became ours president?'

Well, I was deeply flattered. I had never been asked to become president of anything before and my ego was definitely pricked. Furthermore, I had always been a huge fan of the sound of sackbuts. I decided to overlook the fact that Tomas Santos had a poor command of the English language, and I wrote back to him forthwith and accepted his generous offer.

Since then we have become regular correspondents and, although I have not yet had the opportunity to see Wind, String & Faggots (or even meet Tomas himself), I have enjoyed being their president very much and I was recently delighted to learn that the seven concerts they have performed since I came into office have raised over ten pounds for charity (or charty, as Tomas calls it).

I hope you enjoy this, Tomas's first book. I'm sure it will be the first of many. He is a young man (I think) of enormous talent and he has a great eye for picking presidents – and that's something that you cannot say about most authors, now is it?

Editor's acknowledgements

Numerous experts have helped me in the preparation of this book by checking the accuracy of various parts of the manuscript. Any errors that remain are therefore their responsibility.

I am particularly indebted to the following people without whose support, during the gestation of this work, my spirit would have been broken: Gyles Brandreth; Adriano Budiùlo; William Carson; Noam Chomsky; John Cooper; Helen Cumberbatch; Jed Cutler; Jerk Dajmkryss; Steven Elsey; Concetta Fregna; Roberto García; Tony Hawks; Martin Howells; Encarnacion Joder; J. Y. Kelly; John Kirby; Stavros Kolobaras; Jabir Mamhoon; Efraín Maricón; Ken Maycock; Fanny Merkin; Laura Morris; Michelle Nichons; Penny Parker; Marianne Saabye; Alison Sharpe; Paul Smith and Gill Lake at The Triangle; John Thomas; Jo Uttley; Hans Wichser; Charlotte Wolff; and Richard Wolfströme. I send them all my sincere thanks.

T. A. CUTLER
The South Coast, 2004

Prelude
by Tomas Santos

Hello.

When I visited firstly in England all was foreign and the queer native startled me with his tongue. So I was decided to learn of English and I worked well hard all day in the language college and tossed myself onto the mattress every night with exhaust.

Before I came in England I started already speak absolutely English. To be exercised I read the classics book such that Dickens: *Oliver Twit* and L. M. Montgomery: *Anne of Green Bagels*. But in my home land it was not allowed to have the seditious book so I hided them in the hole in my uncle's back passage. I had also some phrase books but they was incomprehending and I made my mind, such that when I would be a flowing speaker English, to wrote a easy learning phrase book for aliens to master also of it. So *Speak Well English* came!

May be it is that you also are newly visiting in UK and can don't speak English. Then this booklet is purpose of you. All pupil should wish he shall got better in the promptly fashion and *Speak Well English* are give you the unique helpment! This notorious guidance book empowers a learning tourist or the apprentice to flourish at once to acquire fluency English, notwithstanding inferior initial knowings.

I am hopefully that many alien will quickly had pleasure from the English tongue and if you study closely you shall at once forget that native ejaculations feel strange in your mouth. Therefore, as the English drinking salute said it: cheerio to your good health, and up your bottoms!

Cardinal vocabularies

Have ever the correctly term up your arm. Simply dive under the category adapted of the banner and you can getting it.

Daily objects
The homestead
The electric comb of tooth
A chemise
The hair rake
The paper water
Your wallet
The cravat
The socks strap
A shoes
A coat
A cold coat
Lavender of toilet
The plume
The rubbing gum
The papers
Some clips
The news paper
The daily book

The sunny couch
Your tablets

The avocations
The physician
The doctor
The alderman
The fire labourers
The servant civilian
The employee
The field broker
The contributor
The counsel
The charlatan
The professor
The police serves and women
The engineer civilian of the
    works
The milk officer

The towns clerk
The fish broker
The dimple master
The master of the fabric
The lattice master
The reader newses
The notable
The postman
The civil lovings
The commercer
The rosary
The cesspool vacuum

Maladies

Tonsils throat
A bad nose
The inflamed suffix
The shattered member
A throat endemic
A fistula mouth
A bad end
Hansen's disease
Febrile hives
Big breaths
Blood weight
Haemorrhage owls

Employ and business

E-mail
Another meeting
World-class intervention enablers
Thinking outside the bogs
High-level backbone process
    tasking
Appraisal
Coffee break
Feedback
Downsizing
Redundance
P45

Cookings

A pocket of cookings
A grocer
A fork
A tractor
A charcoal biscuit
Food hooks
A soup sieve
An grate cheese
A jacknife
Pickled herons
An mixture mushed up

Failure juices
The sausage
The nose of the padre
Thighs
Breasts
Fruits liquidated
Some chocolate fasteners
A catheter

In the stores
A little money
Some bought
Some bought of window
Damage

The vehicle
The car
The gas pedal
The traffic jelly
The window sweeper
Motor road
Eyes cat
A collapsed wheel
A station wagon
A traffic warder
A parking certifcate

A wheel clam
Jack off
The horn
Director the traffics
Hour dash
Carless driving

Home-made animals or a animal
The cat
The smooth cat
The doges
A dress poodle
A litter runt
A pig guineafowl
The business the dog
Lamp column
The cage ape
The vet surgery
A hare
A seeds
A wolfs
An horse
A Leo
Orang
Faecal-ladle

Passtime

Horses ridding
Wrestlers
Stamps acquision
Music
Digging
Macramé
Ferrets
Balling
Anus

Of some nations

Australia
Irish
Of Scotch
Gaul
Flounders
The Americs
Jacobite
Flemmish
Welch
Britsh
Ingress
Brasil
China Syndrome
Malagasy

Garlic
The French
The Belgiums
Missile

Music instuments

Spinet
Chime
Ocarina goose
Outrage
Conch hooters
Toilet webs
The oud
Aluminium whistle keychain
Congalongs
The tarsia
Ba-Hus
Chocolate éclair
Uillean pipes
Music
Viola of the knees

The evenings costume

The black tie
The cummer bund
The silk sockings

The silk pants
The silk hat
The silk gauntlets
Crash helmet

Holidays

Airplane
Sun oils
The slimming pool
The hostel
Germans
Calamari
The reprisal Montezuma
The photos
The sea side
A sand palace
Skin cancer

Of the relations

The sister
The bother
The sun
The daughters
The second cousin
The cousin once displaced
The niece
The self-aligning spherical
    rod-end bearings
The mother
The father
The greatmother
The greatfather
The black sheep
The uncle
The mother-in-lav

Commonplace discourses

The most superlative method to learn of language is jump on the deep end. They realistic dialogues such that are afterwards printed allow the callow pupil to play with his new tongue and lick any problem.

In the restaurant

The UK restaurants shall serve you very old food such
that roasted beef of old England, pig heads eating the
apple, streak and kidney pies, saucy pap, and cock
in wine. You may then end with a spotted dick.
You will be very fed up so enjoy your meal!

Good night, hotelmaster. I have reversed a table.

*Welcome in our restaurant, Sir, your table is for five covers
equipped. The waiter shall here in a minute.*

No, he must attend me at once!

Very good, Sir. He comes now.

Thank, I see him.

What do you want, Mister?

This bread sticks is inferior, boy. I wish another
directly.

Accept this replacements, Sir. Also here is yours menus. Shall you drink?

Get us best wine.

Very good, Sir, the smellier comes quickly. He will make you well drunk!

Tell us, do you have crabs?

Desolately they is not of season.

Well, are yours livestocks cultivated?

Ever.

We are then made up. My sister is on the game; she would take widgeons and otherwise fowls with impact butter in a crisp bacon and we shall begin white baits and then to the 'Coq-bird With Wine & Fireburnt Sauce in a Gallic Mood'. Will you inflame the coq nearby that we shall observe the wonder?

No.

That was a delicious table. I am repleted.

Good news, Sir. Shall you desire more any items?

Kindly ignite my cigar only, waiter, and deliver me the addings check.

My pleasure! I bid you farewell.

Useful sayings in the restaurant

Do you serve faggots?
Take notice – my lady wants stuffing.
Is this a smoke house, my dear fellow?
Toss your plum sauce.

How do your quail, Miss? Are they well burds?

Show me your breasts.

This desert is too much hot. Have you some cold cream?

Cook my goose!

I was served of an old trout. I wish select again inside your
aquarium.

Is this lobster or crap?

I desire one of your hearty fools with hard nuts, if you please.

My salad is wanting, waiter. Put a dress on.

Call me a yellow cab; I have gone blotto!

Did you desire me to pass water, Madam?

Under a barber

The hairs dresser of Great Britain shall wish to cut you very badly, and serve you right too! He is marked by the striped post and, similar to drivers of taxi, all hairs dressers have pleasure to discuss the problems of the world. Relax during he does his toilet on you.

The discourse

Well morning, my hairs expert.

To see you!

Can you strim me?

Unhappily I must cut this gentleman in front of you. But wait in a moment and I shall attend you by and by. You may pursue some the magazine or a news paper in my banquette.

I will him. Oh, bother! These journals are elderly.

Sir, I am yet prepared. Sit you and I should cover you with a membrane. Now what may I do?

Crop my hairs if you please, and toilet me.

Not at all, I can it at once!

Will you shave me also?

With pleasure. Did you saw it the soccer game in the TV chum?

No, I went in Firenze. What squad you endorse?

Manchester Untied!

I understand. Have your completed my hairs even?

See in my looking glass. How like you them?

You have mussed it. Please give me a blow job and wave it.

Very well. Should I anoint you or colour in the grey threads?

Not it! But I would smell nice. Please squirt my tonsure with a odour. In another matter, had you something to the week end?

You rogue, Sir! Here are some. Now must you oblige my moneys.

How many?

Sixteen euros.

Here you were. See you latter.

No doubt.

Useful sayings in the barber

Please stop tickle me.

I never go in another barbers to got my hairs ruined – I come
   here.

Tissue me.

Take caution! You cut on my ear somewhat.

To speak with an old

Many old shall muse of nostalgic. He may have a forgettings memory and folded skin, or thin bones such that he is bent. But be amused of the story of Mr Therm or MacDonald Hobley or starting handles. He may saying always the same, but laugh at him any way.

The discourse

Hello, you old. How was the world like when you are a little boy?

Is it Monday?

Saturday.

Pardon?

It is the week end, Sir. Now, can you tell to me: what is it like when you were juvenile? Did you travel of the horse, for example?

You must speak more loud, you lad. I have got aids in both my ears.

Are you turned on of the ears trumpet?

What did you said? My canals are full of water. I hear only the rushing cataract.

No, the cataract is of your eye globes, is not it?

Pardon me?

Look, I shall increase the noise of your ears instrument. There. Can now you heard me?

Where is my spectacle, boy? All is blur and I see merely clouds.

You have already your lorgnette in your nose.

Och, of hilariously! In due course shall I forgot my head. Tell me, are my tooth at once inside?

Yes, Sir. You have all of it. So shall we begin?

Who are you? What do you want of me?

I have some questions. Remember?

Shoot!

When you were boy were there automobiles or must you mount the horse?

Yes.

Were you ride a penny-farting before the auto was discovered?

His name was Dobbin. He was a comely nag.

Did he galloped?

No. We shot him.

Where?

In the twitten.

Whyever?

He caught glanders.

Oh.

And farcy.

Tsk, how shame.

What are we talking about?

You were to tell me of when you were childish.

Oh my, it was a gold age. Our pleasures were easy. I had merely the hoop and stick for a game, or to laugh at the mad in our asylum, or go to the public hanging with cheese sandwiches. Our chicken gave always good eggs, our pigs made bacon, the linnets and pipits and titlarks chanted in the water meadow, and my brother worked in the sun shine on the farm.

Was he shepherd?

No. He was small boy so they put him inside the machinery to scavenge of chaff and it cutted his arms off.

Oh, what rotten luck. Had you any sister?

Yes. She went mad of the syphilis and her nose fell off.

Are you sure about that?

We had not penicillin, you see. It was harsh. But jolly.

Where did you lived?

In my house.

Of which town? You have some foreign intonations.

Scotchland. I am a McTavish, native of the Trossachs. Here this book displays of all family tartans pattern. Do you wish to look up my kilt?

No. Time is of the effervescence.

Yes, it is tea time. Will you eat of Dundee cake or drink of a wee glass?

Not just now, thanks.

Come, son. You are virile; push me around in the gardens. I shall make a circulation in my bath chair and suck my cakes.

The air is a little cooled, Sir. Shall you require your shawl or drink some linctus?

I will have fortified Jerez in my flask!

Don't be naughty; you are not allowed some alcohols.

You must speak up, lad. I cannot hear a word you said; I am completely dead.

Alright then, zipper your cardigan, Pop.

Oh, heaven! I must needs avail of the water closet.

I shall call nurse at once.

Please hurry.

Useful sayings to speak an old

What have you done of your teeths?
Trousers down first, granddad.
It is time for your pink physic.

In the surgeon's office

The British doctor has the busy sick bay and a lot his patients are dying to visit him. When you go consult a doctor in England do not alarmed if you get a prick with a needle. Also certain doctor in UK are woman, but do not suffer trepidation, merely speak slowly to be understanded.

The discourse

Good day, surgeon. Are you running well?

I am gooding, many thanks. And with you?

Alack, am I indeed out of coloured.

Don't again tell me you are queer.

I am so. I fear to my ails. I have an ague. I have the rupture in my collywobbles. My membranes are corded. I have chopped liver.

My dear patent, you are surely the hyperchondriac. Be of a phlegmatic tendency and I shall test your elements and put my telescope on you.

Doctor, I have a pain in my bottom's hole. Shall you look into it?

We shall see what we see.

Do I wrong nerves? Is my very digestion corrupt?

Settle, Sir, or must you elevate your blood pressings. I shall check your humours. Open widely your tongue that I may cause some analysis. Bend. Cough! Had you incidentally used the ointment I gaved you?

She tasted as a poison. Your remedy has blackened my saddles.

You must not take the medicament inside, you foolish! It is not a swallow. It should for yours exterior surfaces merely. Are you with a pain in the neck?

Yes, the quinsy comes apace and I have the vapours. Will you cup me? Will you leech me?

No, I shall put this repository for a curative.

Not likely! I go polish my lesion with your emolument merely. Then we should confer again.

We agree. You must take care to agitate the vessel and put it. Then will you revive.

That settled it, Doctor. Let me retire and I shall report you soon.

Tell to my receptionist. She shall handle you and appoint you.

I will so, even that she is the impertinent. Let us meeting in a long time. God be with you!

Yes.

Useful sayings in the surgeon's office

I had clenched my head.
I made wind.
I smoke very much – shall I be cured?
I have suffering of my hip's juncture.
I am a bag of nevers, Doctor. Am I in a depression?
My old man is bent and cannot stir. May you exercise the home
    consultations?
I have the flux.
Have you wrote the manuscript for my neurasthenia?
My ear is broken.
I have an ill leg.
A fisherman's friend stuck into my throat and I lost my speech.
Bile stones.

Directing a way

———◆◇◆———

*Very first the things you are probably to have when you
are in the UK are to enquire a directions request.
Avoid to become lost so precisely require, 'Sir, can
you tell me where to go?' He will tell you!
Here is the sample dialect.*

The discourse

Excuse, Madam! I am a strangler in town and I am
get lost. Can you tell where I am?

You are over there, Sir.

Well, yes, but will you guide which way I must
follow to find the National Palace?

*You have gone round the bend somewhat. The National
Palace is near Iceland.*

No, she is in England.

It's a shop!

Oh, I am fool.

Well, Sir, you should not begin your quest from this place. You must start elsewhere.

No, I must from this one.

Very well, your expedition is merely a stone's fling of here. Do you notice the zebra crossing?

I see no animals.

No, he is the road safeness utility, with the streaky beacon.

Oh, aye. I see his balls oscillating.

Cross there firstly and next walk backwards in the broad road. Are you understand?

I have you precisely.

Straightly turn and then go away. At the glebe will you abruptly come by the trivium furcation and you must split yourself where you shall see a pelican crossing.

I do not wish the zoo, Madam. Cease your menageries!

But you must obey the man whom is flashing.

Very well.

When the flasher is become green, traverse the way, pass before the traffic lamps and suddenly you shall come in Ann Summers' tradesmen's entrance.

Pardon me?

It is an sexy emporium in a nutshell.

Oh, such shops are unallowed in my home land. I stiffen!

Anyway, follow in the darkling glebe by the blacksmith's and the quarter crossing would be herewith such that you can't avoid it.

But how if I become completely losed? I shall be in Queer Street.

No, my good fellow, merely succeed your nose and 'Bob's your ankle'.

Well direction, Madam.

With pleasure, loser.

Useful sayings to enquire of your bearing

This chart made Greek for me!
Is the museum in near by?
Do I leave on the primary outlet of the carousel?
Bollards!
Who am I?

Some notable visiting points and relics visiting in London

The Congress of Parliament
Mrs Tussaud's Paraffin Show
Nelson's Pole
Primordial Hill
Winnisters

Inexperienced Park
Piccadilly Ring
Madison Square Gardens
Big Bong

Naturism

━━◆◆◆◆◆◆━━

*During thousands years the Anglian people have turned
the sods. They have animals of hunting, such that: of
pigeons; of badgers; of deers wild; of fishes; and of
peasants. So shoot them or enjoy some grass in the
country or in the park.*

The discourse

The sun flickers this morning, friend, and there is
no currents. Let us wend into the spinney. Will you
coming?

*It is the champion ruse that would produce a good hunger
before ours luncheons; I put the boots.*

The sky is mild; we may light foot boots or a small coat. No hat will required.

I shall carry my bird glasses.

We are arrived. Ho! What is it there? Is it pond?

It is pond. See there many are some corncrake, swan, fishes and otherwise mammals.

Ach! You are silly ass. That is nary the swan. Adopt my glasses – that is the cuck with hers children.

You have reason! It must be here a egg nest. What version is she?

I believe it the mullard: female. Where is the husband?

He gathers, presumably, or hunting food to his's kittens.

No, there is he the man. He was to bathe his feathers in the cataract.

Shall you sketch him?

I forgot it my Conté pencils. But I snap him with my chimera.

Look there by the osiers! Do you see some tits?

Yes, they are female tits. It is a very pleasure. Altogether the birds scream, the bees are fizzling, the waters tickle in the lagoon, and the fowlers smell. It is a natural day.

Oh, hang it! We mused and neglect the hour! It is five-and-twenty to two o'clock yet. Ours luncheon should bespoil.

Let us ran home to join our ladies.

Yes, and make one simply enormous lady!

You are the wag.

So you say.

Useful sayings in the outdoors

Cows have been here.
The rain tumbles.
Shall we kill some animals?
Shut the fence!
Bother! A wasp has again bitten on me.
Did a bird muted on you? Well chance!
There is much muck here!
Let us home at once.

In the church

*Every one English visits to church of Sundays.
The Church England (Anglian Church) has spread
his testicles around a globe, to Africa, Asia, USA and
not Ireland. In winter, English church are freezers.
Put the coat!*

The discourse

God morning, Reverend Father. I am newly to
yours church and I wished to met you.

Welcome in our congregation then.

Your church indeed is vivacious, Vicar; your temples
are bulging.

Yes, my congregations are swollen. What thought you of us?

I enjoyed your gay worship and I was impressed such that your singing was without musical accomplishment.

You are nice to point it; I rest on my choristers!

They are lusty!

Yes, they scream well the hymnal.

Your musicians also appear to be amateur!

What thought you of Miss Jefferson on the organist?

She plays with spunk, Vicar. I shall remember her in my prayers.

I hope also you shall remember the many that are sick of our church.

Indeed – I shall spend in your sick bowl, Vicar.

You are kindly. You know we have numerous clubs that you may involve. For instance, our ladies have cast off clothing of every kind to raise moneys. The Archbishop comes to look at them in the church hall on tomorrow. Will you join him together?

I look towards it. I will come in my best trousers. He indeed is an inquisitive primate.

Shall I request him to put your sister in the club also?

Vicar, I have the worry she shall not like it.

Worry will kill you, my son – let our church help.

Very well. Should I set on fire a tapir?

Not really, merely visit in ours service on Easter and lay an egg on the tabernacle.

I look forward it. God bless, Vicar.

God bless!

Useful sayings for the church

Show me the famous spoiled window of glass.
I have an experience on the road to Domestos.
Have you the surplus surplice?
Tell your prayers.
Tell grace.
Hassocks!
Cassocks!
Evensnog.
Happy-clappy.
The church is kept locked
    at all times.

With the tailor

UK persons look ever sleek in their refinery. A tailor in UK shall never used machinery that tear your clothings – they do it by hand. They are fast also and will stitch you up before you knew what happened. So put your new doublet and spats and do gay things.

The discourse

Hello, tailor!

It is fine to see you, Sir. Come!

It is that I must some altering my costume. May I drop my trousers for a proper seeing to?

With willing, Sir. What is amiss your garment?

I have a discomfort in my fundament; I required more allowance. Check my pants if something is wrong.

Abandon your pants and I shall correct him tomorrow.

But I must had some trouser to wear in a jiffy. Shall you measure me?

I can do you on Thursday.

But I am hasty! I should not wander in the city without trouser. You must execute me in an extremely soon moment.

Very well. Will you have a fit upstairs?

Can it not here? I shall remove my singlet and have a fit in my pants.

OK then, let's have it off and I will discover how big you are in the vestibule.

Ouch! What d.d you? I felt a prick in my bottom.

Forgive it, Sir. I penetrated you erroneously with the bolt of screw.

Blow me! Never matter – show me your threads without delay then I must suddenly went shopping.

Come again in this afternoon and you should had the suite in a stripes fashion.

Have you gone crazy? I should look as a popinjay.

Perhaps then the herring-tweed with a Prince of Wails Check?

That is a excellent idea; I am over the .noon. I shall come again back.

Yes, why don't you go away?

Useful sayings in the tailor

These pants make my wife hot. She requires the loose costume
for street walking.

Coat me!

I wish purchase a brasserie for the medium woman.

Can you make me a coat from my own skin?

Can you increase the tension in my home?

My sister requires the swimmings costume. Please make
suggestive comments.

Belt me!

Sock me!

Boot me!

Fleece me!

Is my shit hanging out?

A breakfast

The completely English breakfast famous is the entire world. You must prove it at once. Delicious!

The discourse

Good morning, land lady.

And so! What you your breakfast?

I should bacons; the egg; put bread fire; beans cooked with the furnace; toast; dark cakes; coffee; juice of orang; and biscuits.

Do you take the sausage?

You put your finger on it.

I have also toadstools, will you like that?

I should eat abundance they.

Will you taste my new dish?

What it?

He called lutefisk of Norge. He is a sawn fish in three parts that rotted twenty days in lime soap and ashes. He then is coddled in salty brines on a simpering temperature and comes with a heavy smelling sauce.

I think I'll give that a miss, if you don't mind. Got any cornflakes?

Not.

Well, just bring to me the others foods, if you please.

I hope I shall pleasure you.

Indeed, I have a hunger.

I will cook thems forthwith.

Yes, Ma'am.

Useful sayings of breakfast

Toast me.
Marmalade solders.
I have jammed my fingers.
Scrambled ovaries.

In the orchestra concert

UK has many musicals such that: The Prannets *by Gustav Holst* or *Elgar's* Enema Variations. *To visit in the concert you may hear wonderful musics when you sit down on your orchestra stalls. So if the bus conductor comes of the stage to wave his arms in the* Air on a G String, *applause him.*

The discourse

What will we listen tonight, Wilfred? I am forgotten.

Here, see the menu, Violet. It will be firstly Flight of the Bumble Wasp, *then* Ride the Valkyries *by Robert Wagner, followed of Handel's* Large.

What becomes after the intromission?

Well, they will do in Haydn strumpet concerto and they finish off Beethoven's Erotica.

At home I am exploring Wagner's *Ring*.

That sounds horrible.

It is sixteen hours, but I like to listen it.

Did you know of English composer Henry Purcell?

I know only his opera *Dildo and Aeneas* conducted of Benjamin Britten.

Do you like The Fairy Queen?

Yes, he was a good conductor.

What of that Miss A. Brevis?

Never heard of her.

Look, Violet. I have not before asked of you, do you perform of the music insurment?

Piano is my forte.

How very lovely.

Shall I give you a little snatch in my apartment subsequently?

You're telling me! Did you know I tooted a wind when I was schooling in county Kent?

That interesting, Wilfred.

Yes, we boys took our instruments out of a hat and I got the horn. But I could not well blow myself and I didn't stand up to examination with the other ones.

Did you matriculate?

We all matriculated together, in Sandwich, near Ham. But I came last because I can don't read music notes.

I can't believe me.

Yus. Unhappily I am delinquent of ability.

But I have heard you titillate the ivories. With the cross hands also!

I was jamming.

You must have a very good ear.

Pardon?

I said you must have a very good ears.

No. I can't tell my Arne from my Elgar.

Aha! Here comes Sir Rattle now. I hope he will get a warm hand on his opening.

Let us give him the clap.

He deserves it.

Useful sayings in the musical concert

Bravo!
Tutti.
Andante molto.
Arco.
Con sord.
Encore.
When's the interval?

To speak with childrens

The childrens are same in the world. The laughter and behaviour with unmade of the hairs. You should amuse a conversation with some rascal in order improved your linguistic capacities.

The discourse

Come, child, do not be childish. Do not mud my floors!

I wish play, Mama.

Very well, nipper, but do not select your nose. Be well bread – you must stroke your tooth and rake your hairs.

Must I polish the face?

Indeed. And give to your large-mother the kissing.

No, she is like the horse's end!

You are scallywag. Not employ this tonality of the tongue with my! How the challenge you speak me such that? Regard your elder and improve them. I shall slipper you. You must be trounced.

Very well, Mother, I am now corrected.

A good boy!

Useful sayings to childrens

Golly gumdrops!
You are no good and will
    amount to nothing.
Cleanse the shoes.
Sit you and shut of mouth!
Who has blown off?

Romance

In England is the art of chivalry. A man must make always the compliment of a lady and hold for her the doors, stand when she comes, and buy rich presents. If she asked: 'Darling, do you liked my new frock?' he must said yes or it will a terrible evening and recrimination. (Note: A gentleman must rise always his hat before he strikes a lady.)

The discourse

I love to you, Olive.

I love to you also, Quentin.

You have a beautiful tooth.

Thank you.

As well you have a beautiful leg.

Just the one?

And the beautiful black hairs.

On my leg?

They tumble on you shoulder.

None on my head then.

Olive!

What?

Did anyone told you have some provocative eyes?

You make overdone the adulation, Quentin. Cease now of your compliments.

But I want to give you one!

Flattery are better to be more few. You try too much hard.

But Olive, you have a lovely chest and your neck looks like a goose.

You mean a swan.

Yes. I shall give you a pearl necklace.

OK, enough already. You are all hot or bothered. Stop now or I must slap your bottom.

You're making it worse. I am overcame of license. I am hypnotized by your nose.

Really?

A man should give a millions dollars to kiss on such a nose.

If I had a million for this nose I'd blow it on myself.

You deserved it. Your waste is narrow, your pelvic griddle is slender, your belly is fair, and your figure is slime.

No, I must be more slimmer. I have too much fat thighs.

Scribble and balderdash! You are very gorgeous.

Thighs apart, you mean.

No. I do not love either completely skinny or fatty legs.

You prefer something in between?

Yes.

You indeed know how make a lady feel sensory, Quentin. I am week of the knees. Come in my bed at once.

Must I take of my pants?

Well, you can not eat of the chocolate with a wrapping on him.

OK, I am ready!

Oh, to goodness' sake! You look an absurd to be in only your balaclava.

I will have it off forthwith.

I thought that was the general idea.

Move you over then, Olive.

Blimey, Quentin. You are more bristles than you look!

Quiet, woman! It is bad conduct to speak with the mouth full up!

Useful phrases for the romance

May I steal a kiss?
Sir, I wish marry your daughter's hand.
Stop yer ticklin', Jock.
These johnnies are past their use-by date.

On an airport

All traveller must go in the airports. If you need informations you shall find the airport staff are all over the place. So prepare these discourse and then you can just go away.

The discourse

Hello, Miss. I am arrived in your terminal, but I must know some knowledge of where I am go. Are you an enquiring person?

No, I am runaway security. You must ask of our informations. They will tell you where to go – they have a reputation for it. Here comes a somebody. She shall make you trip good.

Oh, hello lady. May I probe you?

Yes, I am information. What do you want?

I am going away.

Go on then; I'm not stopping you.

No, you must tell me: is my fly open?

Which number fly is you?

Here, see on my billet. I go to Prussia at 9 clock.

Ah, you have the low-cut airline. It is not now time to get board.

When may I get board?

In a half an hour they undo the plane for your fly. You must make a connective bus in our otherwise terminal. They will take you for a complete ride.

Where shall I leave them?

Try talking to the diver and he will just tell you where to get off. Do you have a case to put?

Yes. I put two suits cases and a handbag.

You must check the baggages forthwith.

I think I will urinate myself first. Where is the rest rooms?

Next to Caffée Latino and Starbucks.

I am about to go.

Have a nice day.

Hello, man. I have come of your another terminal.

Good day, Sir. May I see you passport at this time?

Are you the bag man?

Sir, I am a check-in security. We have the heavy security blanket in the airport at this time. Did you packed your own privates?

Yes.

Do you have gas?

Pardon?

Have you: knifes; gas cookers; killing gun; nail flies; exploding bombs; scissor; electric apparatus, etc.?

Not really.

Fruit?

Pardon me?

Have you fruit?

I have quinces.

Eat them! Have you visited in farms?

I went in the zoological garden.

You may pass to the baggages check-in at this time.

I see.

Have a beautiful vacation.

Well met, check-in lady. Here are my baggage.

Put it on the carrier belt. But, Sir, your details is not righteous. You are illegitimate.

Oh, Lord! How it?

You did not completed the luggage label. Do him and I will tell you where you can stick it!

There. It is done.

You now are well. You may pass out in the flying sector.

Bye.

*

Hello, man. It is a pleasant day.

Passport!

Here she is, friend.

Come on, I haven't got all day! Have you been do your business, or a holiday?

I visited in the zoo – for monkey business. Afterwards I swimmed.

Have they looked in your trunks?

Yes, they have seen it.

Walk inside that inspection scaffold. Put your heavy metals on the drawer. They shall radiograph your handbag.

Thanks heaven! I made no alarum to ring.

You have been clarified. Wait in the antechamber now for your Prussian fly. You may purchase tax-free gods in the terminal shop at Gate Eleven – Elf! She is adjacent the ornamentalized fountain. Why not drop in?

Thanks, buddy.

Useful sayings of the airport

Put the trey-table in a uptight position.
Fatten your seat belt.
This your capitain speaking. We soon will crash in London
    so sit and relax you.
Do not rub me up the wrong way, lady, my dander is up!
Quit farting me about!
I wish speak Stelios!

In the greengrocer's

At every street angle in UK are the cheerful
greengrocer's with his brown paper bag, his wrong
apostrophe, his jolly costermongers song, and his
cauliflower ear. 'Buy my goosegog's; the'yre lovey!' he
scream's all day – it is in his marrow. Follow this
discourse to get serviced with a fruit.

The discourse

Good morrow. Are you a fruit shopkeeper?

Yes, Sir. What may I do you for?

Are you also a vegetable man?

Yes. I am a fruit and a vegetable.

Tell me then, what edible pulp available you?

I have: vine peach's; huckleberrie's; egg fruit; grapefruit's; pomme-pomme's; seabuckthorn berrie's; mango's; melon's; and today we have also mulberrie's.

Do you go round the mulberry bush?

No. We have the fruit's collection of Nine Elm's and I daily exhibition them in pleasing heaps.

You have handsome plum's, my dear fellow.

They are tasty, isn't it!

What of your rhubub's? Are them good of growth?

Yes, Sir. They is ready to eat! We put the horses manure on it.

I put custard on mine.

Deliciously.

I notice such that your rasp berrie's are plenty. His bouquet is sweet indeed, with an exquisite nose.

Pick your own!

Do you got a bag?

Here it, Sir.

Tell me: what are they exotic fruit's your sales clerk's have?

They are ugli.

No. One of they is of pretty girl. Surely those are handsome melon's she has.

If you like them, Sir, you must take a look of her juicy pear.

They are ripe, in my judgement!

Please not squeeze them! The skin become's with smudge's of customer finger.

Regrets! Say, buddy, I would know: are your mandarin's inseminated?

They are liberated of all seed. You may remove also their skin's of easy-peelers.

Good show! I shall select them for to zest my gateaux's ingredient's. As well to that, have you good lemon's?

Are you taking the pith?

I require merely her juices.

Well then, they lemon's are that for which you are looking. They is saturated of juice and will excrete their's elixir with ease. My father also and I make a gurgle with the fluid for the hurtful throat's.

How are your Granny Smith?

Hard!

What about your Cox?

This year they are rotted and shrivellated of a hot summer.

Cor.

Drat it, Sir! You elbowed my arrangement's and my bloody orange's are tumbled of the pavement.

You have unstable piles, O testy costermonger.

I suppose you think your'e funny!

Tell me jolly green grocer, what of your vegetable's?

We have the usual: zucchinis'; cucumber's; plantain's; pimentos'; rutabaga; yam's; celeriac; tomatos; potatos; artichoke's global; and artichoke's Jerusalem.

You have them all of memory, my good merchant?

You think I dont know my onion's?

Do you squash or sprout?

They is not came of this month. The frost had blasted them. Any else?

Have you some cheap roots to made a cheesy vegetable soup?

My swedes are going for a snog. Or were you thinking of some other?

Yes, I need a leek. And a *long* one.

I have a whopper. Let me put it in your sack. Will you take my pulses?

Never. The bean procures me flatus and I always take a pea in the tin can.

Oh.

But I need some okra for make my especial curry. Have you it?

Sir, I have ladies fingers in my back passage. Shall I retrieve you some them?

No.

Goodbye.

Goodbye, darling.

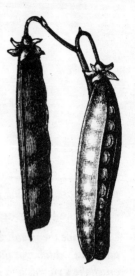

Useful saying's in the greengrocer's

Youv'e got a lovely bunch of coconut's.
When can I have a banana again?
An apple for the teacher.
Cherry ripe, cherry ripe.
Orange's and lemon's.
Strange fruit.

In the hostel

To visit in the another land must you ever settle in the hostel or sleep in the other man's bed. This discourse should help to you to manage speak.

The discourse

Good morning. I am inhabiting the room and I wish some remarks for the director hotel.

Sir, I am at your dispersal.

I left my values here last night but my pass book is vanished. I probed your mistress but she was contemptuous to me. She said if I think she's rude I should see the director. Will you discount me?

Sir, I discount you already.

We improve directly. Now then also is my bidet broken and I cannot receive CNN.

I can direct ours engineer should repair yours bidet in tomorrow or your chambermaid will look into it this morning. What would you?

I will take advantage of the chambermaid!

Is there more?

Merely I wish you would alarm me tomorrow. I shall take my breakfast now from the salon, but in the next morning I should want it at 6 a.m. from a waitress in my bed.

Are you complete?

One furthermore question, please.

Yes?

There is a widow in my shower.

Yes?

I cannot shut her up.

I see.

And she is frigid.

Do you refer the French widow, Sir?

No, the French widow is in my bed room. Her opening is first class. The other is old and stiff and is letting fly always a terrible wind such that I shan't stand for it. She engenders the goose's bumps on my person when I am denuded, and I cannot stick it out.

Look, I shall ask our man to investigate her with his tool after breakfasts. Can you describe this widow so he may locate correctly the one?

She is tiny and coloured and she will not shut up.

My man will fix your window and endeavour so you will satisfied, Sir. Will that enough?

That will for a moment. I am finished. God save the Queen!

I hope so.

Useful sayings in the hostel

Have I received a massage?
That naughty waitress are get the rough
    edge of my tongue.
Give me a bed with excellent servicing
    from your mistress.
At what clock must I evacuate myself?

In the library

The English invented many science, art, law, music, and sophistry. Also the English invented English to write it all in books. Then they hide them in a library so nobod should know where all the ideas are, or read them. Britain has several public library but this did not made any profits! The dialogue underneath shall improve of your book-learning. No talking!

The discourse

Ahoy there, everybody! Three cheers to the pubic library!

Shhhh!

Oh, hello Lady. Your library has the exciting echo.

May I help you, Sir?

Book me.

Pardon?

I want read a book. I am the book worm.

Off you go then.

Well, tell what books you have.

Sir, this the famous reading room of the British Musum. We have quite all the books are published of the English language. What are you looking exactly?

I wish a French book.

Do you know his name?

Mrs Bovary. It is a anecdote by Gustav Flambée of the lady and his husband. It is his *magnum opus* of French letters.

You want it of the aboriginal French?

Naturellement.

Anything else?

If you please.

What?

I wish another French book.

Which is . . . ?

Au Revoir Monsieur Pommes Frites. I will translate him in English for exercise.

Sir, if I may say it, I think you should find he is a French interpretating of the English book Goodbye Mr Chips *of James Hilton.*

Do you have: *The Old Pickwick Shop* or *Nicholas Twist?*

And they are by . . . ?

They is recommended reading books of my language school. Both are of Charles Copperfield.

No.

What of *The Nickleby Notes*; *Sketches by the Hearth*; *American Cricket*; *The Curiosity Carol*; *A Man on the House*; *Times and Chimes*; *A Christmas Rudge*; *The Haunted Son*; *Barnaby Life*; *The Battle of Boz*; *David the Drood*; *Martin Friend*; *A Tale of Two Chuzzlewits*; *Oliver Dombey*; *Great Cities*; *Our Mutual Expectations*; *The Mystery of Edwin Dorrit*; or *Bleak Little Deep Hard Frozen Papers*?

None of it.

Then I should ike made just the photostat for my alien visa. Show me your reproduction equipment and how you like to be turned on?

Sir, I go to the stacks.

Have you the interesting works of Graham Greene: *A Burnt Suit-Case*, *Our Man In A Van*, or *Travels With My Cunt*?

Goodbye.

Thank for your help, Miss.

Useful sayings in the library

This library no good! I am going to Boots.

The penis mightier than the sword.

Is this English grammar book an American-English English grammar book or an English-English English grammar book?

Why did my inter-library loan took two years?

Have you *Jamie's Scratch 'n' Sniff TV Cookery Experience*?

I fondle libraries.

Have you something in a large pint for my grandmother?

Why will the council close you down and sell every books for 50p?

These early colour plates are fantastically valuable. Have you the razor?

Book handlers.

Fahrenheit 451.

Silence!

At the postage office

The postage office may be a meeting plaice of the
village. Go there for the pictures card or to bought
elasticated bands. You can make fun with the elder
peoples of arthritic when you buy your stamps,
and then you can lick them.

The discourse

Good day, my man. Do you speak English?

Very. How shall I help you, Sir?

Are you a mail?

I beg you?

Are you a post?

What do you want exactly?

I must telegraph and I wish send things, but I should pick your brians for I believe my packet is too large.

Put him in the balance.

Here is he. What balance does he make?

He weighs median, Sir. I can handle him with pleasure.

What expenditure shall it?

Where you like your things to go? We will send them in every direction.

In Europe.

Very good. He will amount to seven guineas for air deliverance.

Do it!

You first must nominate your fillings.

They are English gewgaws.

Just fill in this form and I will service that lady from behind.

No, I want more.

What other do you demand?

My French letter is a funny shape. Can you stamp on it correctly?

Have some phlegm, Sir. Our stampings contraption uses the latest methodism.

Very good. I am certain it shall travel with celerity. Here now is my complete form.

No, you must reserve it.

What should I do?

Stick it!

It is stuck. All is now done. May I push my packet in your hole?

Yes.

Until we meet again then!

See you late!

Cheers, mate!

Useful sayings of the postage orifice

Can you envelope me?
I am exhausted of brown papers.
Do you box?
Please lick my gums.
Ribbon me.
I wish to transmit a post.

In the pictures gallery

Many pictures gallery are abundant with painting and decorating. If you like to stare at the nude you could go there. Public exhibitionism is mainly gratuitous in England so why not take advantage of them?

The discourse

We are arrived now in the National Pictures Gallery. What shall we view in the first instance?

I don't care less.

Like you the Victorian century?

Yes. Conduct me that I should view the Impersonators.

Follow in this way then. Here are we. These illustritions are indeed fine. What you think them?

I don't like to notice the brushing marks.

Well, this is *Portrait of the Yellow House* by Van Gogh, and that is his way to painting houses.

Was he insane?

Aye.

And cut his ears off?

Yes, he did.

I think his front door needs repainting.

What you opinion of this self-portrait by Renoir?

Who's it of?

It is of he!

I like more The Gurning Cavalier.

Oh, fair enough.

This nude is well hung.

Yes, indeed. It is by Augustus Egg. This position shows well his assets.

In the label says it: 'Fellow of the Royal Academy, Augustus Leopold Egg'.

Yes, he was a good egg.

You should be on telly.

Shall we have a look in the Bacon room? I should like to view more the modern work.

Very well. We must go through sculptures showroom.

What think you here of this notorious woman?

She has a hole in the guts. This statute was craved in the modern way. I will not it. A child could made it!

It is indeed contemporaneous.

It's Monet for old ropes. Let us buy instead some Salvador Dalí mouse mats in the shop and enjoy the cheesecake in the refractory.

Useful sayings of the pictures gallery

Those are well tickets, isn't it!
What is it supposed to be?
I wish to look at Constables and Sergeants.
This one's brilliant, it looks just like a photograph.
I do not know much of art, but I know of which I like.
Admire you more a dead nature or the shelf-portraits?
This video installation is the work of another charlatan.

At the garage

In England are rough thoroughfares and ill-metalled
byways. Therefore is the vehicle to have a often
check-up with the fitter, who will go all over your car
for a leak, or otherwise. If you are not tanked up on the
highway, AA can give you one for the road. They also
shall test your water and blow up your wheels. This
realism scenario in the motor garage will cause you to
become exercised.

The discourse

Good day, Mr Mechanic. My car is ill. I have drived her into the bay.

Has she sinked?

The *parking* bay in your behind.

Yes, I understood. I merely was ribbing of you, Sir.

Well, be more grave if you will!

OK, don't bite of my head, mate. What is the trouble your car?

My wife drived her merely one week and then she broke down.

Have you been pushing her around?

I dragged her on a rope, after my trailer.

I hope your nuts are secure on your shaft.

Yes, thanks. Can we get on with things?!

Of curse. Shall you describe her?

Well, I suppose so: she is a French model.

Tasty. What colour?

She's white.

Is she fast?

Once upon time she had indeed a reputation of it, but now is she slowing down. She crawls home after the night out and is horrible screechy. She as well has always a gigantic thirst and can put away gallons. She is costing me the fortune!

How old she?

I shall not say it. Is that consequential?

OK, what about her body?

Pardon?

Describe me her body. I will make a picture in the head.

Well, she was long ago sleek, but she is faded and start truly seem her age. She has scratches all over her backside and there is something wrong with her hooter.

Does it make a whistling when she blows it?

You're tell me! Also her spare tyre is unsightly and covered of grease.

Is she starting to smell?

Yes. She gives a foul odour while she climbs the hill to our house.

Does she have gas?

Yes. And she smokes heavy as we driving.

From her pipe?

Yes.

Does she dribble?

She do.

I see. How about when she is idle?

She will make a grinding noise.

As puffin and panting?

It is more such as the gurgle sound when I try to get her going. She used to went like clappers and had an electricity, but her battery seems dried. She has become cold to my touch.

Right. How do you turn her on?

I do it with an old crank. When I put him in the little hole she is always frosty and it take eras before I can turn her over. I put a blanket on her parts at night and I warm up her in the morning with a hot sponge, and rub on her seat with the oily rag.

What she is like under the covers?

She used to get steamed up easy, but now not. Her bottom has a hole in it.

Does she ever have a leak on the floor?

With knobs on! And her boot is jam-packed also of water.

How do you deal it?

I remove her bonnet and clout on her head with a gasket spanner.

Did you think to put her to scraps?

She may old, but I still love her! Her bottom has fallen out, but she demands only a filling and maybe a screw under the arches.

Does she want one in her bottom?

Worth a try. I then will pay her tax and drive her hard away.

Bring her round and push her over my jacking chamber.

I will gather her. You shall hear as I come, for her plates scrape the floors.

Don't fear; I will give her a good servicing.

See you in a small while, then.

Dipstick!

Useful sayings in the garage

My car is broken.
The *Highway Cod* gives the precepts to travel.
Has my big end came off?
If it is not busted, not repair them.
Are you unhinged?
Grease monkeys.
Your sparkle plugs is chafed.
My petrol has run away.
Fill me with gas.
Oh, golly! I put in mistaken diesel.
Oil my change.

To the pub

The pub is the British tradition and unique. Much beer is warm or without bubbles so drink of wine. Always introduce yourself into a woman and give her man the clap on his back. Tell to him: 'Sir, I am enamoured of your girl; how old is it?' Or, 'Hello my old Chinese, are you rich?' Cheers!

The discourse

Good day, bar man. I should take two litres ale and some beef jerky.

Will you put an addings ledger?

No. I shall satisfy you at once. How much guineas will that cost mate?

Linger, I compute him. See there, it shall little money – merely £2.

Thank to you my ogod man. I seat now in the tables and shall speaking this pretty lady. Good night, you pretty lady. I like to come across you. May I seat me or have you reservations?

Not at all, Sir! Sit on my right hand. Come you another land by chance?

Yes, you detected me. I am exotic.

You speak well English even.

By all means. I learn it with the book. She named itself *Speak Well English*. I am now fluid, but it is hard to get my head round your tongue.

I don't blamed you.

Shall you some morsel or a drinks, Miss?

No thank.

Allow me to press you.

Then I give up. I wish a goblet Scottish on the stones and the packet salty and onion potato chips.

Wait in a moment and I come again with mouthfuls. I will buy also one packet smokings.

Oh, not! It should canker my bronichals.

Then drink well.

And with you, comrade.

Useful sayings in the pub

Mine's a large one!

Are you coming down The Cock?

Give me a screw driver.

Cheerio to your good health!

Give me tomato sauce with Worcester juice.

Up your bottoms!

How of it you like that wine?

I think you operate a gay tavern.

Waitress, I will another stein.

At what clock are your pubes open tonight?

Are you smoke?

Time gentlemens, please!

At the village cricket game

The cricket is a sport for Englishmen with very hard balls. It is mysterious for the visitor that English get excitement to see eleven men play with themselves in their white trousers. These discourse will assist to made you understand to the ancient sport.

The discourse

Good afternoon, Vicar. It is warmly in the pavilion. Will you give me a favour to explicate me the laws of the cricket, for I am foxed?

With pleasure, my old fruit. This is the game that my four fathers made fun of themselves! It is easy as falling of a log. You must first two sides. One side is outside on the cricket court and one side shall linger inside the pavilion. One man that is in the side that is inside must go and be in outside, but when he is out he must come in and the another inside man will go out and be in until he is out. When all the outside side are out they shall come in and those that are the inside side must go out and get the outside side that now go in out.

That is clear. But who is this running fellow?

That is Mr Hawker. He is a tosser.

I could agree more!

You observe his balls? They are nine inches of circumference and he may rub them on his trouser or also put spittles on them to be brilliant. In sometimes may he polish 'nose greases' on them so they shall wobble in the air.

Will he then throw him?

He must not throw, he must 'bowl' it. You see he must not jerk under his arm or he will be called 'no balls'. If he will cause the Leg Before Wicket (BMW) the other shall be out and go in.

May a woman play it?

Indeed, Sir. I teach the ladies a lesson. On Friday night I showed them my yorker in the Scout hut.

Did you score, Vicar?

No. They fight like tigers. Mrs Banting handles my googlies with no troubles and Mrs Best also can take a full toss in her sleep. But she is the sporty woman. You know she makes athletic massages to the farmers' rowing club?

Yes, Vicar. I have seen her in the gym, rubbing down their cox.

Careful, you nearly knocked my pint over.

Tell me, Vicar. Why does the doctor arrive always in his hospitals coat?

He is not doctor, you silly, he is the Empire. He will watch and gesticulate his judgements to the scorings board with movements.

Then who is this fellow with gauntlets?

He is the wicked keeper. You observe also the captain has a Short Leg and a Silly behind?

Yes, he has his hand down his pants.

You charlie! He only adjusts his box.

So, when all his men are gone the races each are counted?

Exactly.

How exciting!

Oh, I say! Mr Martin is out for a duckling.

Vicar, please explain me what is 'The Ashes'.

Burnt sticks in a tin. But forgive me, I must put my armour to be the next beater to go in the field.

What is 'the follow-on'?

Excuse me, I want to play badly.

What is a 'dead ball'?

I must go.

What means 'One short'?

Good afternoon!

I hope you will score the goal, Vicar.

You are a fruitcake, Sir.

Useful sayings of cricket

Who is wining?
Did we again lose?
Owzat!
Oh, bother! Bad light stopped play.

At the sea side

—◦◦◦◦◦—

The sea sides of UK is frolicsome and the English are
laughable. Smile at the native who paddled with the
trouser up and the neckerchief on his pate. Put a penny
to see what the butter saw or eat of gelatine cones,
of burghers, and of the infamous English luncheon:
fishes and crisps. But put always the sun shield
to avoid skin canker.

The discourse

Hello, Mr Tourist Officer. What time is Lancashire
open?

We never close.

Will you welcome me then in your town?

Indeed, Sir. This is my town and you are welcome to it.

Why are you so attractive?

Well, we have extremely facilities for the families and the delicious beach for bathe or for sunning, and all is secure. We have handsome live guards and you safely may dip the waters in your swim pants.

Then I shall instruct my sister to make a bikini test in the brine.

Our strong seamen operate also the boat expedition to display our surrounds, or for the fishings. Should she delight in that?

Will she catch crabs?

It cannot be explicit. Our harbour must first enjoy well currents for the crabs to aggregate.

Do you have a sandy bottom?

We have of gravel and of sandy both. Attend me and I shall show you it is clean at once.

Super.

Here, look at my front. See the spectacle. We have the sands; the aquatic memorial; the piddling pool of childrens; manifold feeding kiosks; the candy froth emporium; and confections.

Tasty!

Of our sea shore we have the jackass ride, the bathings, the toilets, and the keck chairs. The swells rush on the beach and many bath in the safe waters. I am always coming in my trunks.

I find that hard to swallow, what with this crud oil on every side.

Look; see there! The men are volleyballing and leaping. They are catching their balls in a jaunty disposition.

The ladies also do recreate in their tiny attire. Oh I say, Madam, what a terrific snatch! I like increasingly your town, mate. She is a bonny environs.

Indeed, the seas are waving, the sun belts down and the peoples are having ecstasy in the water.

But what is leaking of that brown pipe?

It is of no interesting.

Is it ordure?

Let us quick go on the neighbourhood and you shall see such that we experience ever sun shine in ours municipality.

But do you have some of amusements here?

Why, yes. Look of the esplanade; we have multifarious they!

I want to go in your ghost train and look at your ghoulies in the dark.

You shall scream of terror at the hairy monsters. Will you not prefer to come in the bummer cars?

No! I should sick me. Can you are suggest some others pass time?

Take a hike!

I have an ill leg for climbing. I would more like golf on your lynx.

Be my guset. Do you have some man to play with you?

No.

Do you want to play around? I can look after your ball bag.

Ah! Unhappily am I complete rusted of the game and I am badly handicapped.

This is hard work!

What will you do of your holiday, Mr Tourist Officer?

I am going to Masbate for sixteen days.

I beggar your pardon?

It is a sunny aisle of the Philippines.

The Canaries were the last resort for me.

Are you the ornithologist?

No. Notwithstanding, I must fly.

OK then.

Cheers, mate.

Keep it real!

Useful sayings of the sea side

Kiss my quick.
It is scorch.
Anoint my nose.
Who has the break wind?
Who leaves all these beer tins?
Sand is everywhere in my foods.
My ice cream has dissolved.

In the tea shop and café

*Come in, but do not sit at once. Beforehand must you
shake everybody over their coffee. It is done in UK.
In the British café or the 'Olde English Tea Shoppe'
the British had an elaborate ceremony to tea time such
that cream-tea and sconce with battered toasts.
Watch him ever pluck his lumps with a sugars tong
or see as they wash the 'tea pot' and then stand
upside-down on the training boards.*

The discourse

Miss, we are ready to commission our tea.

Yes, Sir. What you want?

Percolade me two cups tea, if you will.

Typhoid or Earl Grey?

What is he?

He is a delicious drinking infused with oils of aromatic bergamot.

Normal.

And for food?

I am ravishing and I could eat a house!

Do you fancy some of gateau perhaps?

May I get crumpet here?

With pleasure, Sir.

Give me six of the best.

Shall I spread them for you, or would you desire some else also?

Well, I was admiring your fantastic baps.

Thank you.

Will you show me your muffins also?

Take a look at these! Are you satisfied?

I love it! But Miss, I cannot removed the hood of my jam pot.

Sir, are you go round the twist?

I have done the twist two times, but he will not become unattached. How then?

Why don't you just push off!

Eureka! It has fallen.

Your tea pot arrives, Sir. May I milk you?

Your jugs are large, Missus.

That is how I may do every body.

I will cream myself. Can you recommend the best tart in your establishment?

Do you want a spotted dick?

Sauce!

Useful sayings in the tea shop

Nice buns, lady!
Give me a tongue sandwich, Madam.
I take a besprinkled fritter.
One lumps or two?
Your self-service is courteous.
Is this tea or just hot water with smell of fruits?
Get your laughing gear round that, girl!

In the work office

———◦◦◦———

If you are an alien you could work of paid vocation in UK if only you had a lawful paper. You may had rewarding duty as a pubic house ash boy, roads cleanser, or baker's girl to baked the bread – or a tart. With fortune may you traduce the English language or go in the office for factotum doings. Here some dialogue of the work office to familiar you.

The discourse

Good morning, Tracy. How was the week end go?

Oh Sharon, I am browned of! I have the dumps. I have lachrymose. I am misery.

Well, I mean that is quite a bit surprise. Say it what the matter. The problem shared is the problem divided.

I am fool. I should listened of your warns, for Colin has unloaded of me. I am abandoned of my suitor.

I said you that he was an cad and a bounder. Is he attached to another, Tracy?

I cannot speak of it or I should weep me.

Place your head on my soldier.

No. I shall master my sentiments and he can just feck of himself!

Do not cuss, Tracy. It is ill of a lady. I sense what ails you. You need something hot inside you.

Yes, I could do with a stiff one.

Take this kerchief and swab you your eyes. Let us got coffees of the machinery.

Very well. What hearsay know you, Sharon, to take my memory away my problemes?

Did you heard, Jameela said Wendy in Finance has the newly girl baby?

What is her name?

Jameela.

No.

Wendy.

No, the suckling tot.

Chardonnay Kylie Beckham Smith. Here's your coffee.

Oh, that is fair nomenclature. What the hell is this?

Well, I pushed of the coffee indicator, but nevertheless came this green soup.

You know, Sharon, mens are similar all them. Ale and curry and the foot ball merely are his pleasure. Never he understands to romance of a lady with candles, cosy dinner or Barry Manilow. He wishes only to rental of the salacious DVD and make the belch contest with his familiars.

Tell me about it. Crumbs! It has quarter of eleven and I should already inspect of Charles's inbox and prepare for his dictations or shall I be in bad odour.

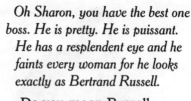

Oh Sharon, you have the best one boss. He is pretty. He is puissant. He has a resplendent eye and he faints every woman for he looks exactly as Bertrand Russell.

Do you mean Russell Crowe?

That's it. Oh, God's blood! He comes now and my facial eye-woad requires of a touch up. I will run away. See you for the lunchbox in a half hour!

OK.

*

Good morning, Sharon. Where has young Tracy disappear so alacrity?

She is a busy body today, Charles. Are you well adjusted to dictate to me?

Of which?

The letters.

Go in my office and I will come in a jiffy.

OK.

Seal the door.

Shall we do it?

Just a movement. Have you completed yet of the yesterday dispatch, Sharon?

Yes. I licked the gums until I am blue and put hunderds stamps.

You are a super asset, Sharon. You lick until the crows came home and I don't know how you stick it. You are a fast lady and you do me well with your short hand.

Charles, I just am a working girl who enjoys it.

At the same time you can keep abreast on my diary.

I can satisfy your normal desires and keep on top of you, Charles, but today I cannot open your files.

You must put 'charles' and then a astérix, two catastrophes and a pound sign. That will my pass word.

OK.

Now, pay close attrition. I dictate of the letter. Are you poised?

Yea.

Right, this it: Dear Sir, I answer to your suggest that we are incompetent of our business. You must know that we are an innovative and client-focused inside-out enabler organization facilitating sticky web-readiness with transforming bespoke turnkey options for growth-centred enterprise brands. Utilizing best practice no-blame strategics and quality-driven benchmark channel implementation, our engineered viral e-services drivers and tailored dot-com action items parent key push-pull strategies off-line to monetize your company's hardball message paradigms going forward. We focus on big-picture base covering and our thinking-outside-the-box and gap-analysis imperatives check below-the-line free-fall and flag best-of-breed incubators at brainstorm stage. Our top-down upscaled magic-bullet solutioning means added client value in incentivizing core-business feedback

input from goal-directed B2B e-tailer throughput optimizing, delivering low-ceiling win-win value-added outputs with cut-to-fit synergistic firewall-friendly SME bandwidthing initiatives, providing showstopper turnarounds and actioning innovative partner-facing growth-based bottom-up scaleable solutions. Building on our track record of iterative short-haul re-envisioneered synergies, and seamless service interoperability, our repurposeable leading-edge thoughtware streaming delivers results-driven tactical future-proof asset value, seamlessly empowering your mission-critical image-enterprise communications with leverageable global knowledge-management and proactive outcome-centred eyeballing deliverables. So I cast off your unmannerly allegations, Sir, and dismiss you as a vexatious alligator. Yours etc. . . . . Got that?

Yes. I shall type up it for you.

Get on with it then.

Useful sayings for the work office

Sing this leaving card.

These appraisals are just crap, aren't they.

I've only been went five minutes and I have me sixty-six new e-mails.

That Stuart has so far up the boss's fundament his merely feet are stick out!

Another restructure?!

Visiting in the sanatorium

All English asylums have a pretty nurse under a sister under a fat matron under a doctor under a sturgeon under a professor. The hospital is the home to thermometers, bed bathing, throat gurgles, drugs, syringes, morphine, and tragic medical accidents. This dialogue has the vocabularies for you to speak when you visit a unhealthy person in the sanatorium hospital.

The discourse

Hello, nurse. Gee Whillikins, it is very much hot coming up those stairs of your! Do not you find it is too much warm in here?

Yes, Sir! I steam as a horse.

You could force cucumbers in your downstairs passage.

Well, we must warm our sick.

Yes, you do not want cold sick.

No.

Look, I am to visit my friend Mr Fleming in Mengele Ward. He had his appendices off. Will you show me into his bed?

The client you wish visit is yet on the trolley. There, by the laundry shoot.

Thank.

A pleasure.

Hello there, Flem. That nurse have well legs, isn't it?

Yes, she is shapeful.

And those stocking they wear really steam my cabbage.

I suppose. So, welcome to my bed, friend. I am pleased of the companion for I became wearied of nothing. Sit you and let us have some quiet intercourse.

This will cheer you. I have bring for you gifts: of pickle eggs, of piglet's tongue, of brown ale, and some cigars.

Conceal it at once! Dr Phibes forbade me smoke.

My vessels are not shipshape as they are ruined of smoking. They make ever tests and today I must have the blood count.

Darcula?

Oh, don't not cause me laugh. It makes pull my sewings and it suffers.

I know. When I went in the hospital it was discovered sugar and albumin in my specimen urines.

Oh dear. Can you make children?

No, but I produce well meringues.

You are pull my legs once more.

Yes. Do they care well you in here, mate? Is it the world-class hospital?

Well, their pharmacy has dispensed with accuracy, and their behaviour leaves me nothing to hope for so I would recommend others.

How are your food?

Not as good. Today I may choose Blood Sausages in a Rich Grave, Intestines Surprise, or the 'healthy option': Nuts Baked Hard on Yeast and Heated Prunes. So I suffer always the green-apple quickstep.

Inconvenient!

Yes, I'm up and down like a bride's nightie.

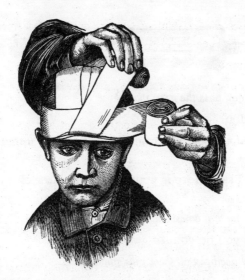

Look here, your offices pals singed this card.

Let me see this. Oh, it is kindly. I see they each have put his name.

All except Clarty Martin. He said you make his skin crawl.

Likewise.

You know, hospitals are smell funny. They give me fear. I had to drinked a couple beer in The Fox to give me of intestinal fartitude.

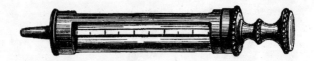

Will you pass the fizzy water?

Pardon?

I must now take my capulets. It is the hour. Please pass the bottle.

Oh, I see. Here is your beverage. How else may I do?

Pass me that emesis basin.

Will you be vomit?

No, I need put all these pills somewhere.

Here are the emesis basin.

You silly billy! That is a specimen vessel. Give me some of the other.

Hey, look! I can spring your bed up or down such that you are bounced.

I think appointment hour is finished, if you don't not mind. I am flagging.

Yes, you look real ill.

Thank you.

Get well soon, friend, and come for a home improvement to be right as ninepence.

Farewell.

Yes, fartwell.

Useful sayings in the sanatoria

Charts.
Blood gases.
Crash trolley.
MRSA.
Necrotising fasciitis.
Bowl movement.

To meet the Queen

In English society or Welch and Scotch or North(ern) Ireland is many way you must to speak to a important VIP (Very Impotant People). This how to have good manners, correctly to touch the fetlock, and address the noble royalties or the upper crust. We begin with to meet the Queen.

The discourse

Hello, Queen.

Hello, man. Why are you are hanging around in the ball room?

It's these hired trousers.

Did you came to listen of the military band?

Yes, their marital music has a prehistoric rhythm.

They musicians are of the Royal African Rifles.

I do not wish controvert you, Queen, but I think they isn't. They are but English paleface mens.

Well, you are looking at their officers; only their privates are black.

Swipe me!

Funny, isn't it?

Funny peculiar, you mean! I see your guests includes tonight also sundry actors.

You're not one of those, are you?

One of those what? I am visiting in England from my home land.

Are you with the Consulate?

No.

Ah. Would you drink of wine or dine some Twiglets? My liveried mens have it.

Did you cook it?

Don't be stupid. My servant did it.

No thanks, Your Majestic. I had a kebab at the bus stop and I am a bit full up.

Have you been here long?

Yes.

Are you learn English?

Very much. This is a nice palace you've got here.

Yes.

She is beautiful as the hanging baskets of Babylon.

Where you live you?

South England. My land lord has two bed rooms and he gave me one in the rear. How about yourself?

I live in these palaces.

They are so much grand. And this masquerade of Prince Philip is the resplendent occasion. It is completely enormous!

Ah yes, the Duke of Edinburgh's balls are the largest in Europe.

And all are dressed so fancy. You look ambrosial in your refinery, Queen. Your diadem sparkles.

But you should see the Price of Wales. His family jewels are the huge ones. He has the biggest stones in the world.

Say, Your Majestic, where is your dogs?

We shut him in the pup house. There is treading foots and they may be injure.

My landlady's pussy has three legs.

Cripes!

A traction engine squashed on it so it now is bald and can drink only soup.

Well, it's been so interesting to learn all about you. Please excuse me.

I know what you mean. I must strain my potatoes also. Where's your kazi?

Speak at the yonder footman and he will take you up the back stairs.

Oh, you are awful! That is a funny joke, Elizabeth. I spilt my sides.

Well, anyway. Until we again should meet.

Vivat Regina.

Respec'.

Useful modes to address VIPs

The king: Your Majestic
The queen: Your Majestic
The knight: Good Knight
The viscount: Good Lord
The arch bishop: Good Gracious
The judge: Your Lud
The earl: Earl Hines
The duke: Duke Ellington
The count: Count Basie
The baronet: Hello

To celebrate of Christmas

Christmas of England start in August with glad cards in
the shop, Yule logs, snowings, Santa Christmas, minces
pie, hot log fires, and the Cratchits. Gay choir boys sing
festival songs such that: O Holy Nightie, Dig Dog
Merrily on High, *and* O Little Town of Bedlam.
*Mayhap will you have a goose from your boss, so put
the muled wine, get a bulge in your stockings, and have
the happy Christmas — for Christ's sake!*

The discourse

Yo, ho, ho! Merry Christmas, Beryl, my darling!

Take of that stupid beard, Dick; you are six days too much soon. Have you been in the pub all morning?

Do not scold at me, Beryl. See, I have bring you some of important beer.

Oh, you really are an end, Dick. Put those bottle in the refridge and come to help me embellishment the tree.

Where are the shinings, the candles, the luminances, the pretty strings, the glister balls, and the glossy trivialities?

In the box.

How shall I hang them? You have no suspenders.

You must dangle it with the filaments, such as last year.

No. I shall supervision the lightings, for I am man.

Your secret is safe with me.

No, it has true. I bring of the bacon; I am the hunter-gather; I put beard on the table; I am *Homo erectus*.

I heard rumours! Look, take the tea cosy of your head and make something to help me.

Oy vay! This tree have many pricks.

Well, it takes to know one, sugar!

No, this have serious, Beryl! There are a bit much lot of pricking spikes. It hurted me. I shall put the gloves.

Just the minute. Those are my ovens glove. Return him at once in the kitchen room, if you don't not mind!

Right then, I shall just suffer hurtful arms to assist you.

And please turn down my forcemeat while you are in there.

How much degree?

Gas mask four.

OK. Is the tree trunk progressed?

Hang on a memento, what now are you drinking?

It is little of gin and I.T.

It's a half a pint!

Beryl, this fairy have bad legs!

Never mind of the fairy's legs. You'd have bad legs, stuck there with six inches of Noble Fir up your jacksie. Get on and inspection those lights.

I shall hang up them.

Do not yet hang of it. Did you assay already thems?

Nay.

You must put him then in the power hole for test his operation.

Right. Make ready of youself; I put the electrocution in it. Three, too, one . . . Oh, mother's love! They are defected. There is no gleam.

Yes, like every year! You need remove each blub one by at a time and put him a good one in his cavity.

Oh, wait now. I have observed what it. They was not clicked of the button in the outlet. So prepare again you. Three, to, one . . .

Oh, God of heaven! What burst in flash? Are you well, Dick? Your head is blackened and your hairs perpendicular and prick up.

It erupted. It discharged. My sock makes smoke and I have severe torment of the arms. But I am hale and yet alive.

Was your hands watery?

Hush now, Beryl. Can you hear of the bells and fruity Christmas songs outdoors.

It perhaps is the Salivation Army in the snow with his lamps on a stick, and brass musicians.

Brass monkeys, you mean.

Hear, Dick. They croon of Hark the Herald Angles Sign! *that was the darling snog of* Big Crosby. *It is absolutely romance of the season to see the snowy, to skate of the pond and admire to the twinkles, to taste of spicy Yule cake, and be of your goodly fellowship.*

Make me then a kiss, Beryl, under the mistle.

No, thank you. You smell of the ashcan.

Yes. I had the sneaky cigar of the pub.

Would you then like some minge pie?
Is hot?
Yes.
Give it.
Merry Xmas, Dick.
And Good Year, Babe!

Useful sayings of Christmas

Jiggle bells.
Three wise men kings.
No rooms in the in.
Baby Jesus is in the manager.
Gold, Frankincest, and myrrh.
Brandy butler.
Your crackers.
More sprouts anyone?
Will somebod please open of a widow.

Of the farms yard

On the farm jolly farmers do not soil themselves.
They have hands to do it. They sit on their corn patch
and rejoice to see another bringing in the sheaves at
Lammastide. The farmer wife made always the cooking
with fresh creams, fatty bacons, and a red face.
With these, and countless severe sun shine, a farmer
has ever the well state of health.

The discourse

Good day, O sanguine farmer. What of your farmstead?

Mind the dung hill, friend . . .

Oh, shucks! Right in it!

You should put the gumboot round here, old boy. How is your sandals?

Forget them. Show me your holding.

Very well. Follow me through my cow shack.

Wow! Your facility is a huge. Tell me, is that grain silo yonder belong you?

No. That is Farmer Guggins of next door. He is bad farmer. His corns are blighted of negligence and his outhouses destitute of the whitewash. He has also an unsightly blue erection in his cabbage bed, which may dangerous.

Bad karma.

Come, I must now supervise the oil-seed harvest and visit in my rape area.

The pasture is indeed mighty yellow.

Yes, that is the way of their efflorescence. We have the rape girls to ready the plants and I have now a machine to deflower them in the field. I can do 17,000 in twenty minutes.

Excuse me, farmer, why is your dog makes a lot yap?

The Guggins boy always pokes his balls through a hole in the hedge and Rover wishes the game so he made snarling.

Has not his father some control of the boy? Does he not follow of the country code to made a example behaviour?

No. Indeed he has not authority fully even of his own animals and his cock is on the rampage again. He has come through the hole in my barn, and he has riddled my cider press with his pecker.

How reprehensible!

This morning he came suddenly through the farmhouse window and made my wife to jump when she was creating pie.

Farmer Guggins?

No, his cock!

You should chop of his head and made him to a soup.

Farmer Guggins?

No, his bird.

Oh.

What other bucolic items must you do today?

Well, I will tup of my rams in the south meadow, comb my silage, and inspect my mangels in the wurzel clamp. Then comes the veterinary to examine at my cow for the udder fly. He is expert; he got a medal for it.

Does he get always a pat on the back?

I suppose. After the lunch I must cut also the coat hairs of the sheep, mow the fields with a tractor, slaughter the fatling, ream my dibber, and lubricate my seed drill in the insemination unit. I must churn the butter, harvest of my plums, and broadcast the germs.

You are very much working. Will you winnow also?

He is yesterday.

I say, my dear fellow, that reminded to me: can you grow me once more a fat bird for Christmas?

Will you have a grouse or shall I goose you again, Sir?

I should prefer take the turkey if is possible.

Yes, I can do it if you will assist me here and now to do some things to my horse.

OK. What his name? He is so pretty I shall do it with pleasure.

Shag the pony.

Pardon?

He is so called. Here, put his harness.

Oh. Right.

Now draw him up the orchard and allow him graze. During the duration, take this auger and bore some tit holes in the bird house of the blasted oak.

Little ones?

Big ones!

Shall the pony bite on me?

No, he is soft. I have castrated his regions. If he became skittish show him this knife.

Good one!

I am now going in the near stable with three of my hands to inseminate the mare. If you are afterwards needful of a thing, you shall find me fencing in the mead.

Touché.

Useful sayings of the farm

Stable the yearling.
Sty the sow.
Henhouse the chicks.
Hutch the rabbit.
Pond the duck.
Butcher the fowl.
Feed the mongeese.
Reap the maize.
Harrow the eggs.
Crop the tuffets.
Clear the excreta.
Wash the udders of the milk maid.
Are you being served?
Scare cow.

On the railroad train

The UK train rumbles all over the place. He was painted of a jolly livery and can go to fast speeds everywhere. But now not. There is no more cheerful buffet car, but speed strictures, cancelling, and delaying. Of steam; of whistles; of brass buttons; of leather seat; of branches lines; and of flowers pot; all now are gone from Dr Beeching. But welcome instead asset strippings, plastic trains, impure graffiti, burned stations, and chaos. All abroad!

The discourse

Good day, Miss. I wish purchase the ticket to go at once in Edinburgh. How much it?

We have leafs on the railroad and the industrial activity of Leicester. Also is there de-railing at Maynard Keynes. The train therefore is cancelled.

I will go then in Birmingham and change.

If you do so I must send you to Coventry.

It is no matter, I shall transfer me. Hurry so.

No. That train is absolutely pre-occupied.

No chairs?

But twenty chairs merely.

Well, OK, I'll have one of that. How much it?

£152.66.

That's rubbery!

Look, they tickets is prime rate, Sir.

Oh, glory! Have you no other?

I have a meagre few of £79. They are second rate.

Why did you not did proffer this one just now?

For Chris's sake! Are you always this rude? Your stage-coach travels away in merely little minutes and you are banding words.

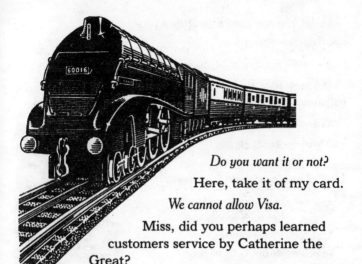

Do you want it or not?

Here, take it of my card.

We cannot allow Visa.

Miss, did you perhaps learned customers service by Catherine the Great?

Please not become acerbic, Sir. My credit engine has gone down on me.

But hows about us poor passengers?

Customers.

So, the most budget fare is £79?

Ah. You did not specific the bargain tariff. I can get you a Virgin for £30.

Just give me the billet and I will ride a Virgin for cash.

Voilà! You see: there is more than one way to sink a cat.

Pshaw!

Sir, your train is now withdrawing of the station.

Oh, cuss!

This window is closing.

Useful sayings on the railroad

Make attention Station Master: your
    bogies rattle such loudly to
    cracked my ear drobes.
The heatment not runs in your
    Pullman car. My feet are cold as
    snow.
These trains once more are again behind
    forty-five minutes.
Porter! Carry of my baggages like a good chap!
Sleepers.
Oh! I have coal smuts on my frock coat.
Filthy washings closet!
Night Mail.

To cooking

To made fine cuisine in the English kitchen you must
learn to some receipts of the native chefs such that
Fanny Craddock! Most favourite are: hot capons with
gelatine; fishes' eggs run away in the meringue nest;
peacock's skull inserted with cream; diabetic winkles on
toast, and faggots on an oily bed. We have put here a
facile recipe to begin you cook lessons. Observe it
precisely and all your servings will look like Fanny's.

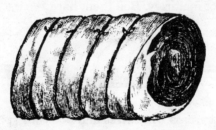

Beef with spit, and lampreys

Take a medium ox.

Put him to the sword.

Draw off his blood in a cauldron with subsequent
purpose.

Remove of his outer vellum and destroy the fatty coat with a scratching brush. Sell this skin to a tanner for his trousers.

Slice away his testicles by a sharp sword. [*The ox, not the tanner. Ed.*]

Open his interiors and dig out his heart, liver, kidney, sweetbreads, lights, bladder, chitterlings, and craw. Mummify this in your salt barrel to make afterwards a pie.

Peel your testicles and put them in a earthen pot. Stick them with some cloves and cover by eighteen pecks of malmsey. Boil them hard.

Tie your carcass with wires and put your spit in him. Lay on honey outside and make a frottage with salts. Roast your body with a vicious flame merely an hour to shut up the vapours.

Take the hot meat and cut him on the kitchen's floor to extremely modest pieces. [*Takes about seven hours. Ed.*]

Toss these meats into a large vessel with a spice and plums.

Add now of the blood and put in a brace of grouse or some rabbits.

Strip fifteen lampreys. Cast them also in the mush.

Add the testicles juice.

Boil yourself uncovered during eleven hours.

Eat it with some roots.

For a wine, choose a one with character of the young lady. She should have a well-picked nose, a robust fruity body, and a rude finish. If she is a little tart, lay her in the cellar.

Post Mortem
by Tomas Santos

Celebrations! You are finish. I take from my hat to you for you now are equipped of a new tongue to have intercourse with any aborigine. From my book you learned to drop your pants at the tailor and have a leak in your soup. Should you now bump on another English somebody, you have felicitous chatter on the tit of your tongue and shall not talk of cross porpoises. If you wish made the toilet in England – and are not know 'am I "gentleman?"' or 'am I "lady"?' – you now can go at once in the rightful cubicle and not fall between two stools. In your vacation, in the hostel, or in the cricket game, you have mastered the knack to introduce yourself, cocksure, into a man or a woman – or even a monarch!

So, at once, opportunity knocks, for all mens esteem opportunity and salute successful knockers. But take careful: do not seem to flaunt yourself or come over everyone like smarty-pants, for the Englishman will scoff a clever Dick. Furthermore, do not buy your friends another cheap languge book that is rubbish, give them *Speak Well English*!

Ultimately, I hope you will success, so cheerio to your good health, and up your bottoms!

Other Michael O'Mara Humour titles